The Green T

by Diane Elson

SCHOLASTIC BOOK SERVICES
NEW YORK · TORONTO · LONDON · AUCKLAND · SYDNEY · TOKYO

ISBN 0 904578 00 3
This edition is published by the International Division of Scholastic Magazines Inc. by arrangement with Dobie Books Ltd.
First Printing ....April 1976
Printed in the U.S.A.

02

ONCE UPON A TIME THERE WAS A GREEN TIGER

At least he always said he was green. And that was because he didn't like his yellow and black stripes.

None of his friends had stripes. He wanted to be like the Crocodile. The Crocodile was green all over.

If, thought the Tiger, I were green all over,
I would be the most beautiful animal in the jungle.
Even more beautiful than Henry the Lion.

And he sighed and looked at
himself in the pool.

"I would be so much more handsome," he murmured, and he sat there all morning just looking at himself in the water.

The Crocodile was lying at the other end of the pool, and he was tired of hearing the conceited Tiger. So he pretended to be asleep and just watched the Tiger out of the corner of his eye.

Soon Henry the Lion arrived at the pool and said, "Hello," to the Tiger whose name, by the way, was Julius after Julius Caesar. But Julius didn't hear him and just went on talking to himself.

So the Lion went to talk to the Crocodile, and they talked about the weather

and the things lions and crocodiles talk about
which make them different from people.
The Crocodile enjoyed talking about eating
people. It was his favourite subject.

But the Lion didn't want to talk about that,
he wanted to talk about the Tiger. He said, "I am
tired of Julius," and that made the Crocodile
stop thinking about eating people

and start thinking about how to cure the Tiger of wanting to be green and the most handsome animal in the jungle.

"We could start singing every time Julius talks about becoming green," said the Crocodile.
"He probably wouldn't notice," said Henry.

“Perhaps we could throw coconuts at him,” said the Lion thinking aloud. But the Crocodile shook his head.

"No," he said, "the only answer is to let him be green and see how much he likes it. I would much sooner be yellow than green."

So they thought of a way to make
the Tiger green.

Julius the Tiger got up early the next morning feeling very discontented. He washed himself and had his breakfast.

Then he walked down to the pool to look at himself again. He was still looking when the Lion arrived.

"Good morning," said Henry, "and how is the yellow and black tiger this morning?"

"The green tiger is very well thank you," answered Julius.

"H-m-m-m," said the Lion, "I have brought you a present."
"Oh," said the Tiger, "is it my birthday?"

"No," said the Lion. And he showed him a tin of green paint and a large paint brush.

The Tiger looked surprised, and the Lion smiled and said, "Now you can be a beautiful green tiger."

The Tiger sat down with a bump and stared at the Lion.

Quickly the Lion picked up the paint brush and dipped it in the green paint.

Starting with the Tiger's whiskers Henry began to make Julius green all over.

The Lion painted the Tiger all morning,

until even his nose, ears, toes, and tail were green.

"There you are," said the Lion standing aside. "Now you are green all over and the most beautiful animal in the jungle."

The Tiger smiled and smiled at the Lion, and thanked him again and again.

Henry did want to laugh. So he said, "Goodbye, I must go and have my lunch now."

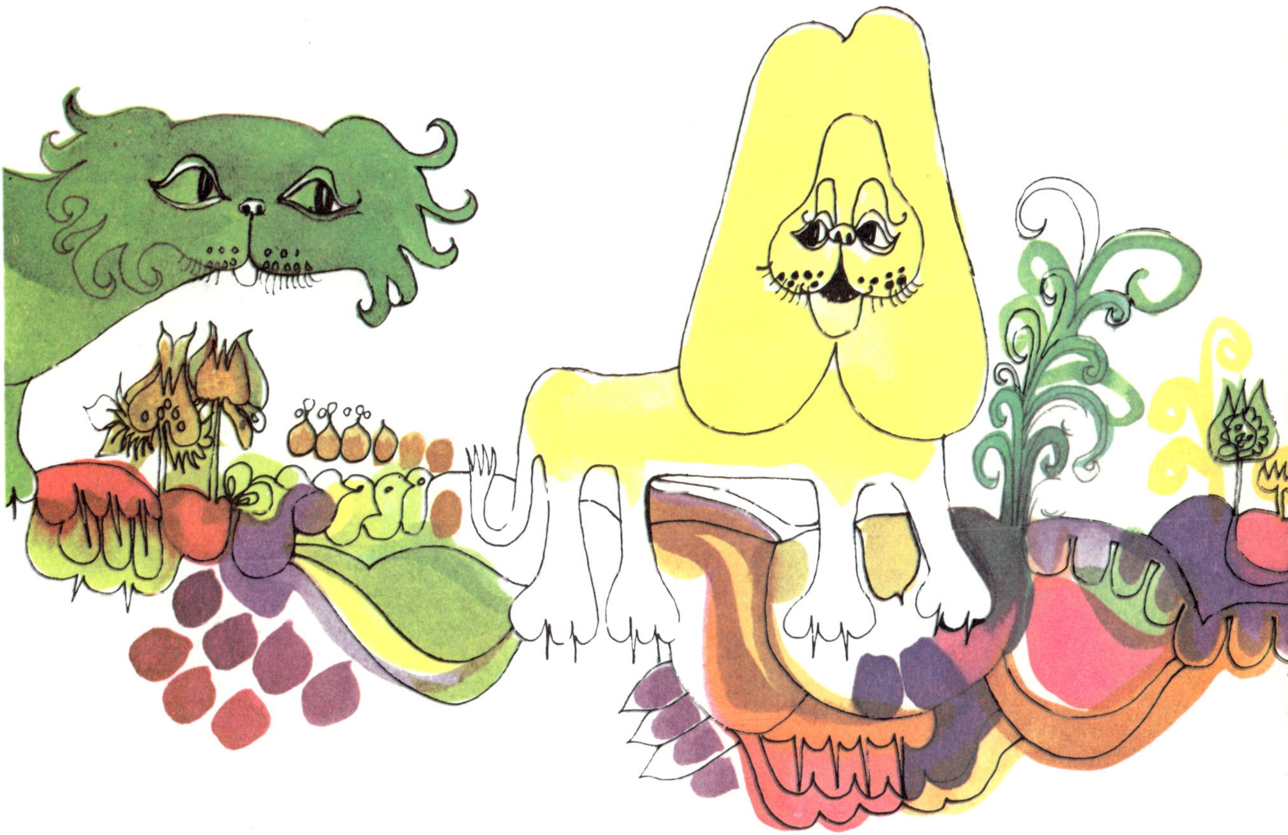

And he left the Tiger alone, now green all over.

He went away laughing to himself, and he was still laughing when he met the Crocodile.

And the Crocodile was still laughing when the Giraffe came to see what they were laughing about.

And they were all still laughing when

the Tiger walked down to the pool to look at himself.

He looked, and looked again, and then again. What a nasty ugly tiger looked back at him from the water!

He stared and couldn't believe his eyes. He wasn't the most beautiful animal in the jungle after all, but the most ugly.

Then he realised it had been a trick and he was very annoyed and very cross.

He was just about to scream with annoyance when he heard laughter coming from the other end of the pool. He looked up and saw

The Lion, the Crocodile and the Giraffe all laughing at him.

He jumped into the pool so that he could swim across and tell his friends what he thought of them.

But forgot that he couldn't swim and in the end he had to be rescued by the Crocodile.

When he had recovered and could look at himself
in the pool again he saw a dripping
yellow and black tiger

and all that remained of the green paint was his green ears.

Julius sighed, for still he wasn't the most beautiful animal in the jungle.